THE ULTIMATE COFFEE AND EXPRESSO COOKBOOK

100 IDEAS TO MAKE THE PERFECT COFFEE-INFUSED RECIPE

ROSEMARY LEE

All rights reserved.

Disclaimer

The information contained in this eBook is meant to serve as a comprehensive collection of strategies that the author of this eBook has done research about. Summaries, strategies, tips and tricks are only recommendation by the author, and reading this eBook will not guarantee that one's results will exactly mirror the author's results. The author of the eBook has made all reasonable effort to provide current and accurate information for the readers of the eBook. The author and its associates will not be held liable for any unintentional error or omissions that may be found. The material in the eBook may include information by third parties. Third party materials comprise of opinions expressed by their owners. As such, the author of the eBook does not assume responsibility or liability for any third party material or opinions. Whether because of the progression of the internet, or the unforeseen changes in company policy and editorial submission guidelines, what is stated as fact at the time of this writing may become outdated or inapplicable later.

The eBook is copyright © 2022 with all rights reserved. It is illegal to redistribute, copy, or create derivative work from this eBook whole or in part. No parts of this report may be reproduced or retransmitted in any reproduced or retransmitted in any forms whatsoever without the writing expressed and signed permission from the author.

TABLE OF CONTENTS

TABLE OF CONTENTS 3

INTRODUCTION 7

COFFEE-INFUSED DESSERTS 8

    1. BERRY TIRAMISU 9
    2. CHICORY CREAM BRULEE 11
    3. MOCHA FONDUE 13
    4. TIRAMISU 15
    5. SPICY ITALIAN PRUNE-PLUM CAKE 18
    6. ITALIAN COFFEE GRANITA 21
    7. HONEY BEE CORTADO 23
    8. COFFEE GRANITE 25
    9. COFFEE GELATO 27
    10. CHOCK FULL OF CHOCOLATE ICE CREAM 29
    11. CHOCOLATE RUM ICE CREAM 32
    12. IRISH COFFEE 34
    13. ICED DOUBLE CHOCOLATE MOUSSES 37
    14. CAPPUCCINO FRAPPÉ 40
    15. FROSTED MOCHA BROWNIES 42
    16. BISQUICK COFFEE CAKE 44
    17. COFFEE GELATIN DESSERT 46
    18. COFFEE MOUSSE 48
    19. COFFEE-COCONUT AGAR DESSERT 52
    20. ITALIAN AFFOGATO 55

COFFEE INFUSED WITH TEA 57

    21. HONG KONG TEA BREWED WITH COFFEE 58
    22. ICED COFFEE TEA 60
    23. MALAYSIAN COFFEE WITH TEA 62
    24. BUBBLE TEA ICED COFFEE 64
    25. COFFEE AND EARL GREY BOBA MOCKTAIL 66
    26. COFFEE-BERRY GREEN TEA 68

COFFEE INFUSED WITH FRUIT 70

27. Raspberry Frappuccino 71
28. Mango Frappe 73
29. Raspberry Coffee 75
30. Christmas Coffee 77
31. Rich Coconut Coffee 79
32. Chocolate Banana Coffee 81
33. Black Forest Coffee 83
34. Maraschino Coffee 85
35. Chocolate Almond Coffee 87
36. Coffee Soda Pop 89
37. Semi-Sweet Mocha 91
38. Viennese Coffee 93
39. Espresso Romano 95

COFFEE INFUSED WITH COCOA 97

40. Iced Mocha Cappuccino 98
41. Original Iced Coffee 100
42. Mocha Flavored Coffee 102
43. Spicy Mexican Mocha 104
44. Chocolate Coffee 106
45. Peppermint Mocha Coffee 108
46. Mocha Italian Espresso 110
47. Chocolata Coffees 112
48. Chocolate Amaretto Coffee 114
49. Chocolate Mint Coffee Float 116
50. Cocoa Coffee 118
51. Cocoa Hazelnut Mocha 120
52. Chocolate Mint Coffee 122
53. Cafe Au Lait 124
54. Italian Coffee with Chocolate 126
55. Semi-Sweet Mocha 128

COFFEE INFUSED WITH SPICE 130

56. Orange Spice Coffee 131
57. Spiced Coffee Creamer 133

58. Cardamom Spiced Coffee 135
59. Cafe de Ola 137
60. Vanilla Almond Coffee 139
61. Arabian Java 141
62. Honey Coffee 143
63. Cafe Vienna Desire 145
64. Cinnamon Spiced Coffee 147
65. Cinnamon Espresso 149
66. Mexican Spiced Coffee 151
67. Vietnamese Egg Coffee 153
68. Turkish Coffee 155
69. Pumpkin Spiced Lattes 157
70. Caramel Latte 159

COFFEE INFUSED WITH ALCOHOL 161

71. Rum Coffee 162
72. Kahlua Irish Coffee 164
73. Bailey's Irish Cappuccino 166
74. Brandy Coffee 168
75. Kahlua and chocolate sauce 170
76. Homemade Coffee Liqueur 172
77. Kahlua Brandy Coffee 174
78. Lime Tequila Espresso 176
79. Sweetened Brandy Coffee 178
80. Dinner Party Coffee 180
81. Sweet Maple Coffee 182
82. Dublin Dream 184
83. Di Saronno Coffee 186
84. Baja Coffee 188
85. Praline Coffee 190
86. Vodka Coffee 192
87. Amaretto Cafe' 194
88. Cafe Au Cin 196
89. Spiked Cappuccino 198
90. Gaelic Coffee 200
91. Rye Whiskey Coffee 202

92. Cherry Brandy Coffee 204
93. Danish Coffee 206
94. Whiskey Shooter 208
95. Good Old Irish 210
96. Bushmills Irish Coffee 212
97. Black Irish Coffee 214
98. Creamy Irish Coffee 216
99. Old Fashioned Irish Coffee 218
100. Cream Liqueur Latte 220

CONCLUSION 222

INTRODUCTION

Whether it's a morning drip or an evening espresso martini, amazing coffee is an art form. This Coffee Recipe Book is your guide to understanding how everything comes together for an artisanal coffee drink.

With 100 different recipes ranging from classic cappuccino to specialty lattes, there's a delicious option for everyone. Easily match the expertise of your favorite cafe, with the perfect mix of the techniques and tools needed to give your daily grind a good home.

Brew up the perfect coffee drink just like a barista—in the comfort of your own home. Whether you like it with milk and sugar, lots of foam, on ice or extra caffeinated, one thing is for sure—we all love our coffee. And most of us take coffee a very specific way. From the simplest (straight and black) to the most complicated (half skinny, half 1% milk extra hot Americano with an extra shot and whipped cream), there seems to be no end to the ways in which we can order our coffee.

COFFEE-INFUSED DESSERTS

1. Berry tiramisu

Ingredients

- 1 1/2 cups brewed coffee
- 2 tablespoons Sambuca
- 1 tablespoon granulated sugar
- 1-pound container mascarpone cheese
- 1/4 cup heavy cream
- 2 tablespoons confectioners' sugar
- Ladyfinger cookies
- Cocoa powder
- 2 cups mixed berries

Directions

a) In a shallow bowl, whisk together 1 1/2 cups brewed coffee, 2 tablespoons Sambuca and 1 tablespoon granulated sugar until the sugar is dissolved. In a separate bowl, whisk together one 1-pound container mascarpone cheese, 1/4 cup heavy cream and 2 tablespoons confectioners' sugar.

b) Using enough ladyfinger cookies to cover the bottom of an 8-inch square baking dish, dip the ladyfingers in the coffee mixture and arrange in an even layer at the bottom of the pan. Spread half of the mascarpone mixture on top. Repeat the two layers. Sprinkle with cocoa powder and 2 cups mixed berries. Refrigerate the tiramisu for at least 2 hours and up to 2 days.

2. Chicory cream brulee

Ingredients

- 1 tablespoon butter
- 3 cups heavy cream
- 1 1/2 cups sugar
- 1 cup Chicory coffee
- 8 egg yolks
- 1 cup raw sugar
- 20 small shortbread cookies

Directions

a) Preheat the oven to 275 degrees F. Grease 10 (4-ounce) ramekins. In a saucepan, over medium heat, combine the cream, sugar and coffee.

b) Whisk until smooth. In a small mixing bowl, whisk the eggs until smooth. Temper the egg yolks into the hot cream mixture. Remove from the heat and cool. Ladle into the individual ramekins. Place the ramekins in a baking dish.

c) Fill the dish with water coming up half of the ramekin. Place in the oven, on the bottom rack and cook until the center is set, about 45 minutes to 1 hour.

d) Remove from the oven and water. Cool completely.

e) Refrigerate until chilled. Sprinkle the sugar over the top, shaking off the excess. Using a hand-blow torch, caramelized the sugar on top. Serve the cream brulee with shortbread cookies.

3. Mocha Fondue

Ingredients

- 8 oz. Semisweet Chocolate
- 1/2 cup Hot Espresso or Coffee
- 3 Tablespoons Granulated Sugar
- 2 Tablespoons Butter
- 1/2 teaspoons Vanilla Extract

Directions

a) Chop chocolate into small pieces and set aside
b) Heat espresso and sugar in fondue pot on low heat
c) Slowly add chocolate and butter while stirring
d) Add Vanilla
e) Optional: Add a splash of Irish Cream
f) To Dip: Angel Food Cake, Apple Slices, Bananas, Strawberries, Pound Cake, Pretzels, Pineapple Chunks, Marshmallows

4. Tiramisu

Servings: 6

Ingredients:
- 4 egg yolks
- ¼ cup white sugar
- 1 Tablespoons vanilla extract
- ½ cup whipping cream
- 2 cups mascarpone cheese
- 30 lady-fingers
- 1½ cups ice cold brewed coffee kept in the refrigerator
- ¾ cup Frangelico liqueur
- 2 Tablespoons unsweetened cocoa powder

Directions

a) In a mixing basin, whisk together the egg yolks, sugar, and vanilla extract until creamy.

b) After that, whisk the whipping cream until firm.

c) Combine the mascarpone cheese and the whipped cream.

d) In a small mixing bowl, lightly fold the mascarpone into the egg yolks and leave aside.

e) Combine the liquor with the cold coffee.

f) Dip the lady-fingers into the coffee mixture immediately. If the lady-fingers get too wet or damp, they will get soggy.

g) Lay half of the lady-fingers on the bottom of a 9x13-inch baking dish.

h) Place half of the filling mixture on top.

i) Place the remaining lady-fingers on top.

j) Place a cover over the dish. After that, chill for 1 hour.

k) Dust with cocoa powder.

5. Spicy Italian prune-plum cake

Servings: 12 servings

Ingredient

- 2 cups Pitted and quartered Italian
- Prune-plums, cooked until
- Soft and cooled
- 1 cup Unsalted butter, softened
- 1¾ cup Granulated sugar
- 4 Eggs
- 3 cups Sifted flour
- ¼ cup Unsalted butter
- ½ pounds Powdered sugar
- 1½ tablespoon Unsweetened cocoa
- Pinch salt
- 1 teaspoon Cinnamon
- ½ teaspoon Ground cloves
- ½ teaspoon Ground nutmeg
- 2 teaspoons Baking soda
- ½ cup Milk
- 1 cup Walnuts, finely chopped

- 2 To 3 tablespoons strong, hot
- Coffee
- ¾ teaspoon Vanilla

Directions:

a) Preheat oven to 350°F. Butter and flour a 10-inch Bundt pan.

b) In a large mixing basin, cream together the butter and sugar until light and fluffy.

c) Beat in the eggs one by one.

d) Combine flour, spices, and baking soda in a sifter. In thirds, add the flour mixture to the butter mixture, alternating with the milk. Only beat to combine the Ingredients.

e) Add the cooked prune-plums and walnuts and stir to combine. Turn into prepared pan and bake for 1 hour in a 350°F oven, or until cake begins to shrink from pan sides.

f) To make the frosting, cream together the butter and confectioners' sugar. Gradually add the sugar and cocoa powder, stirring constantly until completely combined. Season with salt.

g) Stir in a small amount of coffee at a time.

h) Beat till light and fluffy, then add vanilla and decorate the cake.

6. Italian Coffee Granita

Ingredients

- 4 cups water
- 1 cup ground espresso-roast coffee
- 1 cup sugar

Directions:

a) Bring the water to a boil, then add the coffee. Pour the coffee through a strainer. Add the sugar and mix well. Allow the mixture to cool to room temperature.

b) French fry the Ingredients in a 9x13x2 pan for 20 minutes. Using a flat spatula, scrape the mixture (I like to use a fork personally).

c) Scrape every 10-15 minutes until the mixture is thick and gritty. If thick chunks form, puree them in a food processor before returning them to the freezer.

d) Serve with a small dollop of cold cream in a beautiful, chilled dessert or Martini class.

7. Honey bee cortado

Ingredients:

- 2 shots espresso
- 60 ml steamed milk
- 0.7 ml vanilla syrup
- 0.7 ml honey syrup

Directions:

a) Make a double espresso shot.

b) Bring the milk to a boil.

c) Toss the coffee with the vanilla and honey syrups and stir well.

d) Foam a thin layer on top of the coffee/syrup mixture by adding equal parts milk.

8. Coffee granite

Ingredients

- 3 cups freshly made very strong black coffee
- 1/3 cup superfine sugar
- 1/4 teaspoons pure vanilla extract
- 1 cup water, chilled
- 1 cup whipping cream
- 2 Tablespoons toasted hazelnuts

Directions

a) Mix the hot coffee, sugar, and vanilla together. Let cool, stirring occasionally until the sugar has dissolved. Add the chilled water and pour into a freezer container.
b) Freeze until slushy. Lightly break up with a fork, then continue freezing until almost firm.
c) Finely grind most of the nuts and roughly crush the rest. Whip the cream until frothy and fold in the ground nuts. Place in the freezer for the last 15 minutes before serving.
d) Chill 4 to 6 tall glasses. Remove the granita from the freezer and break it up with a fork. Fill the chilled glasses with the coffee ice crystals. Top with a swirl of the iced cream and sprinkle on a few of the crushed nuts. Refreeze no longer than an hour, then serve directly from the freezer.

9. Coffee gelato

Ingredients

- 1 1/4 cups light cream
- 5 egg yolks
- 1/2 cup superfine sugar
- 1 teaspoon pure vanilla extract
- 1 1/4 cups freshly brewed extra-strong espresso

Directions

a) Heat the cream until just beginning to bubble, then cool slightly.

b) In a large heatproof bowl, beat the egg yolks, sugar, and vanilla until thick and creamy. Whisk in the hot cream and coffee, and then place the bowl over a pan of gently simmering water. Stir constantly with a wooden spoon until the custard just coats the back of the spoon.

c) Remove the bowl from the heat and let cool. When completely cooled, pour into an ice cream maker and process according to the manufacturer's Directions, or use the hand-mixing method. Stop churning when it is almost firm, transfer to a freezer container, and leave in the freezer for 15 minutes before serving, or until required.

d) This gelato is delicious fresh, but it can be frozen for up to 3 months. Take out 15 minutes before serving to soften slightly.

e) Makes about 1 1/4 pints

10.   Chock Full of Chocolate Ice Cream

Ingredients

- 3 ounces unsweetened chocolate, coarsely chopped
- 1 (14 ounce) can sweetened condensed milk
- 1 1/2 teaspoons vanilla extract
- 4 tablespoons unsalted butter
- 3 egg yolks
- 2 ounces' semisweet chocolate
- 1/2 cup strong black coffee
- 3/4 cup granulated sugar
- 1/2 cup light cream
- 1 1/2 teaspoons dark rum
- 2 tablespoons white crème de cacao
- 2 cups heavy cream
- 2 ounces unsweetened chocolate, finely grated
- 1/4 teaspoon salt

Directions

a) In double boiler, melt 3 ounces unsweetened chocolate. Add milk, stirring until smooth. Stir in vanilla extract and remove from heat.

b) Cut butter into four equal pieces and add, one piece at a time, constantly stirring until all butt has been incorporated. Beat yolks until light and lemon colored.

c) Gradually stir in chocolate mixture and continue stirring until smooth and creamy. Set aside.

d) In double boiler, heat 2 ounces' semisweet chocolate, coffee, sugar and light cream. Stir constantly until smooth. Stir in rum and crème de cacao and allow mixture to cool to room temperature.

e) Combine both chocolate mixtures, heavy cream, grated unsweetened chocolate and slat in large bowl. Pour mixture into canister of ice cream freezer and freeze according to manufacturer's Directions.

11.   Chocolate Rum Ice Cream

Ingredients

- 1/4 cup water
- 2 tablespoons instant coffee
- 1 (6 ounce) package semisweet chocolate chips
- 3 egg yolks
- 2 ounces' dark rum
- 1 1/2 cups heavy cream, whipped
- 1/2 cup slivered almonds, toasted

Directions

a) In a small saucepan, place sugar, water and coffee. Stirring constantly, bring to a boil and cook for 1 minute. Place chocolate chips in a blender or food processor, and with the motor running, pour the hot syrup over and blend until smooth. Beat in egg yolks and rum and cool slightly. Fold chocolate mixture into whipped cream, then pour into individual serving dishes or a bombé dish. Sprinkle with toasted almonds. Freeze.

b) To serve, remove from freezer at least 5 minutes before serving.

12.   Irish Coffee

Ingredients

- 1 cup whole milk
- 1½ tablespoons instant coffee or espresso powder
- ⅔ cup brown sugar, packed
- 1 large egg
- 3 large egg yolks
- ¼ cup Irish whiskey
- ½ teaspoon vanilla extract
- 2 cups heavy cream

Directions

a) Combine milk, instant coffee, and sugar in a medium saucepan. Cook over medium heat, stirring to dissolve the sugar, until mixture comes to a simmer.

b) Whisk together egg and egg yolks in a large bowl. When the milk mixture comes to a simmer, remove from heat and very slowly stream it into the egg mixture to temper it while whisking constantly.

c) When all the milk mixture has been added, return it to the saucepan and continue to cook over medium heat, stirring constantly, until the mixture has thickened enough to coat the back of a spoon, 2 to 3 minutes. Remove from heat and stir in whiskey, vanilla, and cream.

d) Cool milk mixture to room temperature, then cover and refrigerate until well chilled, 3 to 4 hours, or overnight. Pour chilled mixture into an ice cream maker and freeze as directed.

e) Transfer ice cream to a freezer-safe container and place in the freezer. Allow it to firm up for 1 to 2 hours before serving.

13.   Iced double chocolate mousses

Ingredients

- 3 to 4 Tablespoons very hot milk
- 1 (1/4-oz.) envelope unflavored gelatin
- 1 1/2 cups white chocolate chunks
- 4 Tablespoons (1/2 stick) unsalted butter
- 2 large egg whites
- 1/2 cup superfine sugar
- 1/2 cup finely chopped dark chocolate (you want to keep some texture)
- 1/2 cup heavy cream, lightly whipped
- 1/2 cup Greek-style yogurt
- 18 chocolate-covered coffee beans or raisins
- 1 teaspoon unsweetened cocoa powder, sifted

Directions

a) Sprinkle the gelatin onto the hot milk and stir to dissolve. If necessary, microwave for 30 seconds to help it dissolve. Melt the white chocolate and butter gently until smooth. Stir in the dissolved gelatin and set aside to cool, but don't let it firm up again. Whisk the egg whites stiffly, then gradually whisk in the sugar and fold in the dark chocolate.

b) Carefully fold together the cooled white chocolate, whipped cream, yogurt, and egg whites. Spoon the mixture into 6 individual molds, or one large mold, lined with plastic wrap for easy unmolding. Neatly flatten the tops. Cover and freeze for 1 to 2 hours or overnight.

c) To serve, loosen the top edges with a small knife. Invert each mold onto a serving plate and wipe with a hot cloth, or gently ease the mousse out with the plastic wrap. Return the mousses to the freezer, until ready to eat. Serve with chocolate-covered coffee beans or raisins and a light sifting of powdered chocolate.

14. Cappuccino frappé

Ingredients

- 4 Tablespoons coffee liqueur
- 1/2 cup coffee gelato
- 4 Tablespoons rum
- 1/2 cup heavy cream, whipped
- 1 Tablespoons unsweetened cocoa powder, sifted

Directions

a) Pour the liqueur into the base of 6 freezer-proof glasses or cups, and chill well or freeze.
b) Prepare the gelato as directed until partly frozen. Then whisk in the rum with an electric mixer until frothy, spoon immediately over the frozen liqueur, and freeze again until firm but not hard.
c) Pipe the whipped the cream over the gelato. Sprinkle generously with cocoa powder and return to the freezer for a few minutes until you are absolutely ready to serve.

15. Frosted Mocha Brownies

Ingredients

- 1 c. sugar
- 1/2 c. butter, softened
- 1/3 c. baking cocoa
- 1 t. instant coffee granules
- 2 eggs, beaten
- 1 t. vanilla extract
- 2/3 c. all-purpose flour
- 1/2 t. baking powder
- 1/4 t. salt
- 1/2 c. chopped walnuts

Directions

a) Combine sugar, butter, cocoa and coffee granules in a saucepan. Cook and stir over medium heat until butter is melted. Remove from heat; cool for 5 minutes. Add eggs and vanilla; stir until just combined.

b) Blend in flour, baking powder and salt; fold in nuts. Spread batter in a greased 9"x9" baking pan. Bake at 350 degrees for 25 minutes, or until set.

c) Cool in pan on a wire rack. Spread Mocha Frosting over cooled brownies; slice into bars. Makes one dozen.

16. Bisquick Coffee Cake

Ingredients

Coffee Cake:
- 2 cups Bisquick mix
- 2 tablespoons sugar
- 2/3 cup milk
- 1 egg

Cinnamon Streusel Topping:
- 1 cup Bisquick mix
- 2/3 cup brown sugar lightly packed
- 2 teaspoons ground cinnamon
- 1/4 cup unsalted butter

Directions

For the Streusel Topping
a) In a medium mixing bowl, whisk together Bisquick mix, brown sugar, and cinnamon.
b) Add diced butter. Use your hands to crumble the butter into the dry mixture.

For the Coffee Cake
c) Preheat oven to 350°F. Line an 8×8-inch baking dish with parchment paper or grease it. Set aside.
d) In a large mixing bowl, combine Bisquick mix, sugar, milk, and egg using a spatula. Scrape the bowl down.
e) Pour the cake batter into the prepared baking dish and smooth out.
f) Sprinkle streusel topping evenly over batter.
g) Bake for 20-25 minutes or until a toothpick inserted in the center comes out clean.
h) Let it cool in the pan for 20 minutes before cutting. Serve and enjoy!

17. Coffee Gelatin Dessert

Servings: 5

Ingredients

- ¾ cup white sugar
- 3 (.25 ounce) envelopes unflavored gelatin powder
- 3 cups hot brewed coffee
- 1 ⅓ cups water
- 1 tablespoon lemon juice
- 1 cup sweetened whipped cream for garnish

Directions

a) In a saucepan, stir together the sugar and gelatin. Mix in hot coffee and water. Cook over low heat, stirring frequently until the gelatin and sugar have completely dissolved. Remove from heat, and stir in lemon juice. Pour into a 4 1/2 cup mold.

b) Refrigerate until set, at least 6 hours or overnight. Serve with whipped cream.

18. Coffee Mousse

Servings: 4 people

Ingredients

- 2 1/2 Tablespoons Caster Sugar
- 4 Eggs
- 3/4 cup + 2 Tablespoons Heavy Cream
- 3 Tablespoons Instant Coffee Powder
- 1 Tablespoons Unsweetened Cacao Powder
- 1 teaspoon Gelatin Powder
- 1 Tablespoons Instant Coffee Powder and Cacao Powder, mixed - optional, to finish the mousse

Directions

a) Separate the Egg Yolks and Whites. Place the Egg Yolks in a large bowl and the Whites in the bowl of you Mixer. Set aside.

b) Place the Gelatin Powder in a small bowl with the Cold water, mix and set aside to soak.

c) Add the Caster Sugar to the Egg Yolks and whisk until foamy and lighter in color.

d) Place the Heavy Cream, Instant Coffee Powder and Cacao Powder in a small saucepan and heat it up on low heat until the powders have dissolved, occasionally stirring. Don't let the cream boil.

e) Pour the hot Heavy Cream over the Egg Yolk and Sugar while beating. Whisk well, then transfer back into the saucepan on low heat. Keep whisking until the cream starts to thicken, then directly remove from the heat and transfer back into a large, clean bowl.

f) Add the re-hydrated Gelatin to the cream and whisk well until completely integrated. Set aside to cool down fully.

g) While the cream is cooling down, start whipping the Egg Whites to get stiff peaks.

h) When the cream is cool, gently fold in the Whipped Egg Whites in 3 to 4 times. Try not to overwork the cream.

i) Pour the Coffee Mousse into individual cups or jars and place in the fridge to set for at least 2 hours.

j) Optional: when ready to serve, sprinkle some Instant Coffee Powder and Cacao Powder over the mousses to finish them.

19. Coffee-Coconut Agar Dessert

Serves: 4 servings

Ingredients

- 1 1/2 cups unsweetened coconut milk, regular or low-fat
- 1 cup milk
- 1 cup granulated sugar, divided
- 2 tablespoons agar powder, divided
- 1 teaspoon salt
- 2 tablespoons instant coffee granules
- 3 cups water

Directions

a) Add coconut milk, milk, 1/4 cup of sugar, 1 tablespoon of agar powder, and salt in 1-quart saucepan; whisk the mixture together and bring it to a hard boil on medium-high heat, being careful not to let the liquid boil over. After the coconut milk mixture has boiled hard for 30-40 seconds, remove the saucepan from the stove.

b) Pour the coconut milk mixture into the mold(s) of your choice. Allow it to cool.

c) Meanwhile, whisk together the remaining 3/4 cup sugar, 1 tablespoon agar, instant coffee, and water in another saucepan and bring it to a hard boil over medium-high heat. Once the mixture has boiled for 30-40 seconds, remove the saucepan from the stove.

d) Check to see whether the coconut agar layer has hardened. You don't want it to be completely solid; otherwise the two layers will not stick together and slide off one another when you serve the dessert. With your finger, touch on the surface of the coconut agar layer lightly to see if there's some resistance on the surface. If so, holding the saucepan as close to the surface of the coconut layer as possible, very gently pour the coffee layer on top of the previous layer.

e) Let the agar set. This should take about 40 to 45 minutes at room temperature and 20 minutes in the refrigerator.

20.   Italian Affogato

Servings 1 serving

Ingredients
- 2 scoops vanilla ice cream high quality
- 1 shot espresso
- 1 tablespoon nut or coffee liqueur (optional)
- dark chocolate, for grating on top

Directions

a) Brew an espresso (one per person). Scoop 1-2 scoops of vanilla ice cream into a wide glass or bowl and pour over a shot of espresso.

b) Pour 1 tablespoon of nocino nut liqueur or your liqueur of choice over the ice cream and grate over a little dark chocolate.

COFFEE INFUSED WITH TEA

21. Hong Kong Tea Brewed with coffee

Ingredients

- 1/4 cup black tea leaves
- 4 1/2 cups brewed coffee
- 5-8 tablespoons sugar
- 3/4 cup half and half

Directions

a) First brew your black tea leaves in 4 1/2 cups of water. While the tea is steeping, brew your coffee with your preferred method. Make sure both the tea and coffee are fairly strong!

b) When the coffee and tea are ready, combine them in a large bowl or carafe. Stir the sugar into the coffee/tea mixture and add the half and half. Stir thoroughly and serve!

c) This makes 8-10 servings depending on mug size. You can also serve this tea chilled or with ice!

22. Iced Coffee Tea

Ingredients

- coffee
- mild tea
- ice
- creamer optional
- sugar optional

Directions

a) Place coffee K-cup insert into machine. Add ice to cup or glass. Place tea bag horizontally on top of ice to allow brewed coffee to stream through tea bag as it pours. Allow to steep for a few seconds after brewing has stopped. Press tea bag, taking care not to burst bag, and remove from glass and discard.

b) Add creamer or sugar, if desired.

23. Malaysian Coffee with Tea

Ingredients

- 1¾ cup (438 ml) water
- 9 teaspoons (18 g) loose leaf Ceylon black tea
- ⅓ cup (67 g) Turbinado Sugar
- 1⅔ cups (417 ml) evaporated milk
- 1½ cups (375 ml) strong coffee, hot

Directions

a) In a pot, combine water with the tea leaves. Over medium heat, bring to a boil, reduce heat to low and simmer; 5 minutes. The tea should be quite dark.

b) Remove pot or turn off heat. Immediately stir in the Turbinado Sugar until sugar is mostly dissolved; 1 minute.

c) Stir in the evaporated milk. Place the pot back onto medium heat. Bring mixture to a boil, reduce heat to low and simmer; 3 minutes.

d) Strain tea mixture using a fine-mesh sieve lined with cheesecloth, or remove tea bags, if using.

e) Pour in the hot coffee; mix thoroughly.

24. Bubble tea iced coffee

Ingredients

- Ice cubes
- Your favourite coffee, enough brewed for 4 cups
- 3/4 cup quick-cooking tapioca pearls
- 1/2 cup whole milk
- 1/2 cup condensed milk
- Bubble tea straws

Directions

a) Stash your pre-brewed coffee in the refrigerator to cool completely—a few hours or overnight is best.

b) Cook the tapioca pearls according to package instructions. (Don't boil them until you're just about ready to serve—they harden fast.) Let cool in a bowl of cold water.

c) Transfer and divide tapioca into four empty glasses. Pour in cold coffee.

d) In a jug, gently whisk together milk and condensed milk. Divide evenly into coffee glasses (ooh, look how pretty it all swirls!).

e) Top with a couple ice cubes, stick in a straw, and serve pronto.

25. Coffee and Earl Grey Boba Mocktail

Ingredients

- 4 ounces Chameleon Cold-Brew Vanilla Coffee Concentrate
- 3 ounces Earl Grey tea
- 2 ounces' floater (milk beverage of your choice)
- Tapioca pearls (Boba) coated in honey or sugar
- Dash of cardamom sprinkled on top

Directions

a) Prepare boba and coat with honey or sugar.

b) Brew Earl Grey Tea and chill.

c) Cover bottom of glass with boba and some of the sugar.

d) Combine Chameleon Cold-Brew Vanilla Coffee Concentrate and Earl Grey.

e) Pour over boba.

f) Top with cream or milk beverage of your choosing.

g) Sprinkle cardamom over top and enjoy!

26. Coffee-Berry Green Tea

Ingredients

- 1 green-tea bag
- 1/3 cup coffee-fruit drink (such as Kona or Bai brands)
- 1 teaspoon grated orange zest
- Cinnamon sticks
- 1 teaspoon honey
- 3 basil leaves

Directions

a) In a large mug, add a green tea bag to 6 oz. boiling water.

b) Add coffee-fruit drink and orange zest. Use cinnamon sticks to stir in honey.

c) Tear basil leaves and add to tea. Steep, covered, for 5 minutes. Remove tea bag. Serve hot.

COFFEE INFUSED WITH FRUIT

27. Raspberry Frappuccino

Ingredients:
- 2 cups crushed ice cubes
- 1 1/4 cups-extra strong brewed coffee
- 1/2 cup of milk
- 2 Tablespoons vanilla or raspberry syrup
- 3 Tablespoons chocolate syrup
- Whipped Cream

Directions
a) Combine ice cubes, coffee, milk and syrups in a blender.
b) Blend until nicely smooth.
c) Pour into chilled tall serving mugs or soda fountain glasses.
d) Top with whipped cream, drizzle chocolate and raspberry syrup on top.
e) Add a maraschino cherry if desired

28. Mango Frappe

Ingredients:
- 1 1/2 cups of Mango, cut up
- 4-6 Ice Cubes
- 1 cup of milk
- 1 Tablespoons Lemon Juice
- 2 Tablespoons of sugar
- 1/4 teaspoons of Vanilla Extract

Directions
a) Place the cut Mango into the freezer for 30 minutes
b) Combine Mango, milk, sugar, lemon juice and vanilla in a blender. Blend until smooth.
c) Add ice cubes and process until cubes are smooth as well.
d) Serve immediately.

29. Raspberry Coffee

Ingredients:
- 1/4 cup of Brown Sugar
- Coffee grounds for a 6 cup pot of regular coffee
- 2 teaspoons of Raspberry Extract

Directions
a) Place raspberry extract into the empty coffee pot
b) Place brown sugar and coffee grounds in coffee filter
c) Add the 6 cups of water to the top and brew the pot.

30.   Christmas Coffee

Ingredients:
- 1 pot of coffee (10-cup equivalent)
- 1/2 cup sugar
- 1/3 cup water
- 1/4 cup unsweetened cocoa
- 1/4 teaspoon cinnamon
- 1 pinch grated nutmeg
- Whipping cream for topping

Directions
a) Prepare pot of coffee.
b) In a medium sauce pan, heat water to a low boil. Add sugar, cocoa, cinnamon and nutmeg.
c) Bring back to a low boil for about a minute - stirring occasionally.
d) Combine coffee and cocoa/spice mixture and serve topped with whipped cream.

31.   Rich Coconut Coffee

Ingredients:
- 2 cups Half-and-half
- 15 oz. Can cream of coconut
- 4 cups Hot brewed coffee
- Sweetened whipped cream

Directions
a) Bring half-and-half and cream of coconut to a boil in a saucepan over medium heat, stirring constantly.
b) Stir in coffee.
c) Serve with sweetened whipped cream.

32.   Chocolate Banana Coffee

Ingredients:
- Make a 12 cup pot of your regular coffee
- Add 1/2-1 teaspoon of Banana Extract
- Add 1-11/2 teaspoons of cocoa

Directions
a) Combine
b) So simple...and perfect for a house full of guests

33. Black Forest Coffee

Ingredients:
- 6 oz. Fresh brewed coffee
- 2 Tablespoons Chocolate syrup
- 1 Tablespoon Maraschino cherry juice
- Whipped cream
- Shaved chocolate
- Maraschino cherries

Directions
a) Combine coffee, the chocolate syrup, and cherry juice in a cup. Mix well.
b) Top with whipped cream the chocolate shavings and a cherry or 2.

34. Maraschino Coffee

Ingredients:
- 1 cup of Black coffee
- 1 oz. Amaretto
- Rediwhip Whipped topping
- 1 Maraschino cherry

Directions
a) Fill coffee mug or cup with hot black coffee. Stir in the amaretto.
b) Top with rediwhip whipped topping and a cherry.

35. Chocolate Almond Coffee

Ingredients:
- 1/3 cup Ground coffee
- 1/4 teaspoons Freshly ground nutmeg
- 1/2 teaspoons Chocolate extract
- 1/2 teaspoons Almond extract
- 1/4 cup Toasted almonds, chopped

Directions
a) Process nutmeg and coffee, add extracts. Process 10 seconds longer. Place in bowl and stir in almonds. Store in refrigerator.
b) Makes 8 six ounce servings. To brew: Place mix in filter of an automatic drip coffee maker.
c) Add 6 cups water and brew

36.   Coffee Soda Pop

Ingredients:
- 3 cup Chilled double-strength coffee
- 1 Tablespoon Sugar
- 1 cup Half and half
- 4 Scoops (1 pint) coffee ice cream
- 3/4 cup Chilled club soda
- Sweetened whipped cream
- 4 Maraschino cherries,
- Garnish-chocolate curls or cocoa

Directions
a) Combine the coffee and sugar blend in the half and half.
b) Fill 4 tall soda glasses halfway with the coffee mixture
c) Add a scoop of ice cream and fill the glasses to the top with the soda.
d) Garnish with the whipped cream, chocolate or cocoa.
e) Great treat for parties
f) Use a decaf for parties with youngsters

37. Semi-Sweet Mocha

Ingredients:
- 4 oz. Semisweet Chocolate
- 1 Tablespoon Sugar
- 1/4 cup Whipping Cream
- 4 cup Hot Strong Coffee
- Whipped Cream
- Grated Orange Peel

Directions
a) Melt chocolate in a heavy saucepan over low heat.
b) Stir in sugar and whipping cream.
c) Beat in coffee using a whisk, 1/2 cup at a time; continue until frothy.
d) Top with whipped cream and sprinkle with grated orange peel.

38. Viennese Coffee

Ingredients:
- 2/3 cup dry instant coffee
- 2/3 cup sugar
- 3/4 cup powdered non-dairy creamer
- 1/2 teaspoons cinnamon
- Dash each of ground allspice, cloves, and nutmeg.

Directions
a) Mix all ingredients together and Store in air tight jar.
b) Mix 4 teaspoons with one cup hot water.
c) This makes a wonderful gift.
d) Place all ingredients in a canning jar.
e) Decorate with a ribbon and hang tag.
f) The hang tag should have the mixing instructions typewritten on it.

39. Espresso Romano

Ingredients:
- 1/4 cup Fine Ground Coffee
- 1 1/2 cups Cold Water
- 2 strips of Lemon Peel

Directions
a) Place ground coffee in the filter of a drip coffee pot
b) Add water and brew according to machine brewing instructions
c) Add lemon to each cup
d) Serve

COFFEE INFUSED WITH COCOA

40. Iced Mocha Cappuccino

Ingredients:
- 1 Tablespoons Chocolate syrup
- 1 cup Hot double espresso or very strong coffee
- 1/4 cup Half-and-half
- 4 Ice cubes

Directions
a) Stir the chocolate syrup into the hot coffee until melted. In a blender, combine the coffee with the half-and-half and the ice cubes.
b) Blend at high speed for 2 to 3 minutes.
c) Serve immediately in a tall, cold glass.

41. Original Iced Coffee

Ingredients:
- 1/4 cup Coffee; instant, regular or decaffeinated
- 1/4 cup Sugar
- 1 liter or quart of cold Milk

Directions
a) Dissolve instant coffee and sugar in hot water. Stir in 1 liter or quart of cold milk and add ice. For mocha flavor, use chocolate milk and add sugar to taste.
b) Dissolve 1 Tablespoon of instant coffee and 2 teaspoons sugar in 1 Tablespoon hot water.
c) Add 1 cup of cold milk and stir.
d) You can sweeten with a low calorie sweetener instead of sugar

42. Mocha Flavored Coffee

Ingredients:
- 1/4 cup Non-dairy creamer dry
- 1/3 cup Sugar
- 1/4 cup Dry instant coffee
- 2 Tablespoons cocoa

Directions
a) Place all ingredients in mixer, beat at high until well blended. Mix 1 1/2 Tablespoons spoons with a cup of hot water.
b) Store in air tight jar. Such as a canning jar.

43. Spicy Mexican Mocha

Ingredients:
- 6 Ounces Strong Coffee
- 2 Tablespoons Powdered Sugar
- 1 Tablespoons Unsweetened ground chocolate powder
- 1/4 teaspoons Vietnamese Cassia Cinnamon
- 1/4 teaspoons Jamaican Allspice
- 1/8 teaspoons Cayenne Pepper
- 1-3 Tablespoons Heavy Cream or half and half

Directions
a) In a small bowl, mix all dry Ingredients together.
b) Pour the coffee in a large mug, stir in the cocoa mix, until smooth.
c) Then add the cream to taste.

44. Chocolate Coffee

Ingredients:
- 2 Tablespoons Instant coffee
- 1/4 cup Sugar
- 1 dash Salt
- 1 oz. Squares unsweetened chocolate
- 1 cup Water
- 3 cup Milk
- Whipped cream

Directions
a) In saucepan combine coffee, sugar, salt, chocolate, and water; stir over low heat until chocolate has melted. Simmer 4 minutes, stirring constantly.
b) Gradually add milk, stirring constantly until heated.
c) When piping hot, remove from heat and beat with rotary beater until mixture is frothy.
d) Pour into cups and sail a dollop of whipped cream on the surface of each.

45. Peppermint Mocha Coffee

Ingredients:
- 6 cups Freshly Brewed Coffee
- 1 1/2 cups of Milk
- 4 ounces of Semi-Sweet Chocolate
- 1 teaspoons Peppermint Extract
- 8 Peppermint Sticks

Directions
a) Place coffee, milk, chocolate in a large saucepan on low heat for 5-7 minutes or until chocolate has melted, mixture is heated through, stir occasionally.
b) Stir in the peppermint extract
c) Pour into mugs
d) Garnish with a peppermint stick

46. Mocha Italian Espresso

Ingredients:
- 1 cup Instant Coffee
- 1 cup Sugar
- 4 1/2 cups Non Fat Dry Milk
- 1/2 cup Cocoa

Directions
a) Stir all ingredients together.
b) Process in a blender until powdered.
c) Use 2 Tablespoons to one small cup of hot water.
d) Serve in espresso cups
e) Makes about 7 cups of mix
f) Store in a tight fitted lidded jar.
g) Canning jars work well for coffee storage.

47. Chocolata Coffees

Ingredients:
- 1/4 cup Instant espresso
- 1/4 cup Instant cocoa
- 2 cups Boiling water-it's best to use water that has been filtered
- Whipped cream
- Finely shredded orange peel or ground cinnamon

Directions
a) Combine coffee and cocoa. Add boiling water and stir to dissolve. Pour into demitasse cups. Top each serving with whipped cream, shredded orange peel and a dash of cinnamon.

48. Chocolate Amaretto Coffee

Ingredients:
- Amaretto coffee beans
- 1 Tablespoons Vanilla extract
- 1 teaspoons Almond extract
- 1 teaspoons Cocoa powder
- 1 teaspoons Sugar
- Whipped Cream to Garnish

Directions
a) Brew coffee.
b) Add Vanilla and Almond Extract1 teaspoons cocoa and 1 teaspoons sugar per cup.
c) Garnish with whipped cream

49. Chocolate Mint Coffee Float

Ingredients:
- 1/2 cup Hot Coffee
- 2 Tablespoons Crème de Cacao Liqueur
- 1 Scoop Mint Chocolate Chip Ice Cream

Directions

a) For each serving combine 1/2 cup coffee and 2 Tablespoon
b) s of the liqueur.
c) Top with a scoop of ice cream.

50. Cocoa Coffee

Ingredients:
- 1/4 cup Powder Non Dairy Creamer
- 1/3 cup Sugar
- 1/4 cup Dry Instant Coffee
- 2 Tablespoons Cocoa

Directions
a) Place all ingredients in a blender, blend on high until well blended.
b) Store in an air tight canning jar.
c) Mix 1 1/2 Tablespoons with 3/4 cup hot water

51. Cocoa Hazelnut Mocha

Ingredients:
- 3/4 oz. Kahlua
- 1/2 cup Hot Hazelnut Coffee
- 1teaspoons Nestle Quick
- 2 Tablespoons Half and Half

Directions
a) Combine all ingredients.
b) Stir

52. Chocolate Mint Coffee

Ingredients:
- 1/3 cup Ground Coffee
- 1 teaspoons Chocolate Extract
- 1/2 teaspoons Mint Extract
- 1/4 teaspoons Vanilla Extract

Directions
a) Place coffee in blender.
b) In a cup combine extracts, add extracts to coffee.
c) Process until mixed, just a few seconds.
d) Store refrigerated

53. Cafe Au Lait

Ingredients:
- 2 cup Milk
- 1/2 cup Heavy cream
- 6 cups Louisiana coffee

Directions
a) Combine milk and cream in saucepan; bring just to a boil (bubbles will form around edge of pan), then remove from heat.
b) Pour small amount of coffee in each coffee cup.
c) Pour remaining coffee and hot milk mixture together until cups are about 3/4 full.
d) Skim milk can be substituted for whole milk and cream.

54. Italian Coffee with Chocolate

Ingredients:
- 2 cups Hot Strong Coffee
- 2 cups Hot Traditional Cocoa - try Hershey's brand
- Whipped Cream
- Grated Orange Peel

Directions
a) Combine 1/2 cup coffee and 1/2 cup cocoa in each of the 4 mugs.
b) Top with whipped cream; sprinkle with grated orange peel.

55. Semi-Sweet Mocha

Ingredients:
- 4 oz. Semisweet Chocolate
- 1 Tablespoons Sugar
- 1/4 cup Whipping Cream
- 4 cup Hot Strong Coffee
- Whipped Cream
- Grated Orange Peel

Directions
a) Melt chocolate in a heavy saucepan over low heat.
b) Stir in sugar and whipping cream.
c) Beat in coffee using a whisk, 1/2 cup at a time; continue until frothy.
d) Top with whipped cream and sprinkle with grated orange peel.

COFFEE INFUSED WITH SPICE

56. Orange Spice Coffee

Ingredients:
- 1/4 cup Ground coffee
- 1 Tablespoons Grated orange peel
- 1/2 teaspoons Vanilla extract
- 1 1/2 Cinnamon sticks

Directions
a) Place coffee and orange peel in a blender or food processor.
b) Stop processor long enough to add the vanilla.
c) Process 10 seconds more.
d) Place mixture in a glass pitcher with the cinnamon sticks and refrigerate.

57. Spiced Coffee Creamer

Ingredients:
- 2 cups Nestlé's quick
- 2 cups powdered coffee creamer
- 1/2 cups Powdered sugar
- 3/4 teaspoons Cinnamon
- 3/4 teaspoons Nutmeg

Directions
a) Mix all ingredients together and store in an airtight jar.
b) Mix 4 teaspoons with one cup of hot water

58. Cardamom Spiced Coffee

Ingredients:
- 3/4 cup Ground Coffee
- 2 2/3 cups of Water
- Ground Cardamom
- 1/2 cup Sweetened Condensed milk

Directions
a) Brew coffee in a drip style or percolator coffee maker.
b) Pour into 4 cups.
c) To each serving add a dash of Cardamom and 2 Tablespoons of condensed milk.
d) Stir
e) Serve

59. Cafe de Ola

Ingredients:
- 8 cups of Filtered Water
- 2 small Cinnamon Sticks
- 3 Whole Cloves
- 4 ounces of Dark Brown Sugar
- 1 Square of Semisweet Chocolate or Mexican Chocolate
- 4 ounces Ground Coffee

Directions
a) Bring the water to a boil.
b) Add the cinnamon, cloves, sugar and chocolate.
c) Bring to a boil again, skim off any foam.
d) Reduce the heat to low and DO NOT ALLOW IT TO BOIL
e) Add the coffee and allow steeping for 5 minutes.

60. Vanilla Almond Coffee

Ingredients:
- 1/3 cup ground Coffee
- 1 teaspoons Vanilla Extract
- 1/2 teaspoons Almond Extract
- 1/4 teaspoons Anise Seeds

Directions
a) Place coffee in a blender
b) Combine remaining Ingredients in a separate cup
c) Add the extract and seeds to the coffee in the blender
d) Process until combined
e) Use the mixture as usual when brewing coffee
f) Makes 8-6 ounce servings
g) Store unused portion in refrigerator

61. Arabian Java

Ingredients:
- 1 pint of Filtered Water
- 3 Tablespoons of coffee
- 3 Tablespoons of Sugar
- 1/4 teaspoons of Cinnamon
- 1/4 teaspoons of Cardamom
- 1 teaspoon of Vanilla or Vanilla Sugar

Directions
a) Mix all ingredients into a saucepan and heat until foam gathers on top.
b) Do not pass through a filter.
c) Stir before serving

62. Honey Coffee

Ingredients:
- 2 cups Fresh Coffee
- 1/2 cup of Milk
- 4 Tablespoons of Honey
- 1/8 teaspoons Cinnamon
- Dash Nutmeg or Allspice
- Drop or 2 of Vanilla Extract

Directions
a) Heat Ingredients in a saucepan, but do not boil.
b) Stir well to combine Ingredients.
c) A delightful dessert coffee.

63. Cafe Vienna Desire

Ingredients:
- 1/2 cup Instant coffee
- 2/3 cup Sugar
- 2/3 cup Non-fat powered milk
- 1/2 teaspoons Cinnamon
- 1 pinch Cloves -adjust to taste
- 1 pinch Allspice-adjust to taste
- 1 pinch Nutmeg-adjust to taste

Directions

a) Mix all ingredients together
b) Use a blender to blend into a very fine powder. Use 1 tablespoon per mug of hot filtered water.

64. Cinnamon Spiced Coffee

Ingredients:
- 1/3 cup Instant coffee
- 3 Tablespoons Sugar
- 8 Whole cloves
- 3 Inches stick cinnamon
- 3 cup Water
- Whipped cream
- Ground cinnamon

Directions

a) Combine 1/3 cup instant coffee, 3 tablespoons sugar, cloves, stick cinnamon, and water.
b) Cover, bring to boiling. Remove from heat and let stand, covered, about 5 minutes to steep.
c) Strain. Pour into cups and top each with spoonful of whipped cream. Add a dash of cinnamon.

65. Cinnamon Espresso

Ingredients:
- 1 cup Cold water
- 2 Tablespoons Ground espresso coffee
- 1/2 Cinnamon stick (3" long)
- 4 teaspoons Crème de Cacao
- 2 teaspoons Brandy
- 2 Tablespoons Whipping cream, chilled Grated semisweet chocolate to garnish

Directions

a) Use your espresso machine for this or really strong coffee with a small amount of Filtered water.
b) Break a cinnamon stick into small pieces and add to the hot espresso.
c) Allow to cool 1 minute.
d) Add crème de cacao and brandy, and stir gently. Pour into demitasse
e) Cups. Whip the cream, and float some cream on top of each cup. Garnish with grated Chocolate or chocolate curls.

66. Mexican Spiced Coffee

Ingredients:
- 3/4 cup Brown sugar, firmly packed
- 6 Cloves
- 6 Julienne slices orange zest
- 3 Cinnamon sticks
- 6 Tablespoons. Real brewed Coffee

Directions

a) In a large saucepan, heat 6 cups of water with the brown sugar, cinnamon sticks, and cloves over moderately high heat until the mixture is hot, but do not let it boil. Add the coffee, bring the mixture to a boil, stirring occasionally, for 3 minutes.

b) Strain the coffee through a fine sieve and serve in coffee cups with the orange zest.

67.　Vietnamese Egg Coffee

Ingredients:
- 1 egg
- 3 teaspoons of Vietnamese coffee powder
- 2 teaspoons of sweetened condensed milk
- Boiling water

Directions

a) Brew a small cup of Vietnamese coffee.
b) Crack an egg and discard the whites.
c) Put the yolk and the sweetened condensed milk in a small, deep bowl and whisk vigorously until you end up with a frothy, fluffy mixture like the one above.
d) Add a tablespoon of the brewed coffee and whisk it in.
e) In a clear coffee cup pour in your brewed coffee, and then add the fluffy egg mixture on top.

68. Turkish Coffee

Ingredients:
- 3/4 cup Water
- 1 Tablespoons Sugar
- 1 Tablespoons Pulverized Coffee
- 1 Cardamom Pod

Directions

a) Bring water and sugar to a boil.
b) Remove from heat-add coffee and cardamom
c) Stir well and return to heat.
d) When coffee foams up, remove from heat and let grounds settle.
e) Repeat twice more. Pour into cups.
f) The coffee grounds should settle before drinking.
g) You can serve the coffee with the cardamom pod in the cup-your choice

Turkish Coffee Tips

h) Must always be served with foam on top
i) You can request that your coffee be ground for Turkish Coffee-it is a powder consistency.
j) Do not stir after pouring into cups as the foam will collapse
k) Always use cold water when preparing
l) Cream or milk is never added to Turkish Coffee; however, sugar is optional

69. Pumpkin Spiced Lattes

Ingredients:
- 2 tablespoons canned pumpkin
- 1/2 teaspoon pumpkin pie spice, plus more to garnish
- Freshly ground black pepper
- 2 tablespoons sugar
- 2 tablespoons pure vanilla extract
- 2 cups whole milk
- 1 to 2 shots espresso, about 1/4 cup
- 1/4 cup heavy cream, whipped until firm peaks form

Directions

a) Heat the pumpkin and spices: In a small saucepan over medium heat cook the pumpkin with the pumpkin pie spice and a generous helping of black pepper for 2 minutes or until it's hot and smells cooked. Stir constantly.

b) Add the sugar and stir until the mixture looks like a bubbly thick syrup.

c) Whisk in the milk and vanilla extract. Warm gently over medium heat, watching carefully to make sure it doesn't boil over.

d) Carefully process the milk mixture with a hand blender or in a traditional blender (hold the lid down tightly with a thick wad of towels!) until frothy and blended.

e) Mix the drinks: Make the espresso or coffee and divide between two mugs and add the frothed milk.

f) Top with whipped cream and a sprinkle of pumpkin pie spice, cinnamon, or nutmeg if desired.

70. Caramel Latte

Ingredients:
- 2 ounces' espresso
- 10 ounces' milk
- 2 tablespoons home-made caramel sauce plus more for drizzling
- 1 tablespoon sugar (optional)

Directions
a) Pour the espresso into a mug.
b) Place the milk in a wide glass or glass jar and microwave for 30 seconds until it is very hot but not boiling.
c) Alternatively, heat the milk in a saucepan over medium heat for about 5 minutes until very hot but not boiling, watching it carefully.
d) Add the caramel sauce and sugar (if using) to the hot milk and stir until they dissolve.
e) Using a milk frother, froth the milk until you don't see any bubbles and you have a thick froth, 20 to 30 seconds. Swirl the glass and lightly tap it on the counter repeatedly to pop the larger bubbles. Repeat this step as needed.
f) Using a spoon to hold back the foam, pour the milk into the espresso. Spoon the remaining foam on top.

COFFEE INFUSED WITH ALCOHOL

71. Rum Coffee

Ingredients:
- 12 oz. Fresh ground coffee, preferably chocolate mint, or Swiss chocolate
- 2 oz. Or more 151 Rum
- 1 Large scoop whipped cream
- 1 oz. Baileys Irish Cream
- 2 Tablespoons Chocolate syrup

Directions
a) Fresh grind the coffee.
b) Brew.
c) In a large mug, put the 2+ oz. of 151 rum in the bottom.
d) Pour the hot coffee into the mug 3/4 of the way up.
e) Add the Bailey's Irish Cream.
f) Stir.
g) Top with the fresh whipped cream and drizzle with the chocolate syrup.

72. Kahlua Irish Coffee

Ingredients:
- 2 oz. Kahlua or coffee liqueur
- 2 oz. Irish Whiskey
- 4 cup Hot coffee
- 1/4 cup Whipping cream, whipped

Directions
a) Pour one-half ounce coffee liqueur in each cup. Add one-half ounce Irish Whiskey to each
b) cup. Pour in steaming freshly-brewed hot coffee, stir. Spoon two heaping
c) tablespoonful of whipped cream on top of each. Serve hot, but not so hot you scorch your lips.

73. Bailey's Irish Cappuccino

Ingredients:
- 3 oz. Bailey's Irish Cream
- 5 oz. Hot coffee -
- Canned dessert topping
- 1 dash Nutmeg

Directions
a) Pour Bailey's Irish Cream into a coffee mug.
b) Fill with hot black coffee. Top with a single spray of dessert topping.
c) Dust dessert topping with a dash of nutmeg

74. Brandy Coffee

Ingredients:
- 3/4 cup Hot Strong Coffee
- 2 ounces of Brandy
- 1 teaspoons Sugar
- 2 ounces Heavy Cream

Directions
a) Pour the coffee into a tall mug. Add the sugar and stir to dissolve.
b) Add the Brandy and stir again. Pour the cream, over the back of a teaspoon while holding it, slightly above the top of the coffee in the cup. This allows it to float.
c) Serve.

75. Kahlua and chocolate sauce

Ingredients:
- 6 cups Hot coffee
- 1 cup Chocolate syrup
- 1/4 cup Kahlua
- $\frac{1}{8}$ teaspoons Ground cinnamon
- Whipped cream

Directions
a) Combine coffee, chocolate syrup, Kahlua, and cinnamon in a large container; stir well.
b) Serve immediately. Top with whipped cream.

76. Homemade Coffee Liqueur

Ingredients:
- 4 cup Sugar
- 1/2 cup Instant coffee - use filtered water
- 3 cup Water
- 1/4 teaspoons Salt
- 1 1/2 cup Vodka, high-proof
- 3 Tablespoons Vanilla

Directions
a) Combine sugar and water; boil till sugar dissolves. Reduce heat to simmer and simmer 1 hour.
b) LET COOL.
c) Stir in vodka and vanilla.

77. Kahlua Brandy Coffee

Ingredients:
- 1 ounce of Kahlua
- 1/2 ounce of Brandy
- 1 cup Hot Coffee
- Whipped Cream for topping

Directions
a) Add Kahlua and brandy to coffee
b) Garnish with the whipped cream

78. Lime Tequila Espresso

Ingredients:
- Double shot of espresso
- 1 shot of White Tequila
- 1 fresh lime

Directions
a) Run a slice of lime around the edge of an espresso glass.
b) Pour a double shot of espresso over ice.
c) Add a single shot of White Tequila
d) Serve

79. Sweetened Brandy Coffee

Ingredients:
- 1 cup Freshly Brewed Coffee
- 1 oz. Coffee Liqueur
- 1 teaspoons Chocolate Syrup
- 1/2 oz. Brandy
- 1 Dash Cinnamon
- Sweet Whipped Cream

Directions
a) Combine coffee liqueur, brandy, chocolate syrup and cinnamon in a mug. Fill with freshly brewed coffee.
b) Top with whipped cream.

80. Dinner Party Coffee

Ingredients:
- 3 cup Very hot decaffeinated Coffee
- 2 Tablespoons Sugar
- 1/4 cup light or dark Rum

Directions
a) Combine very hot coffee, sugar and rum in heated pot.
b) Double as needed.

81. Sweet Maple Coffee

Ingredients:
- 1 cup Half-and-half
- 1/4 cup Maple syrup
- 1 cup Hot brewed coffee
- Sweetened whipped cream

Directions
a) Cook half-and-half and maple syrup in a saucepan over medium heat. Stirring constantly, until thoroughly heated. Do not allow mixture to boil.
b) Stir in coffee, and serve with sweetened whipped cream.

82. Dublin Dream

Ingredients:

- 1Tablespoons Instant coffee
- 1 1/2 Tablespoons Instant hot chocolate
- 1/2 oz. Irish cream liqueur
- 3/4 cup Boiling water
- 1/4 cup Whipped cream

Directions
a) In an Irish coffee glass, place all ingredients except for the whipped cream.
b) Stir until well mixed, and garnish with whipped cream.

83. Di Saronno Coffee

Ingredients:
- 1 oz. Di saronno amaretto
- 8 oz. Coffee
- Whipped cream

Directions
a) Blend Di Saronno Amaretto with coffee, then top with whipped cream.
b) Serve in Irish coffee mug.

84. Baja Coffee

Ingredients:
- 8 cup Hot water
- 3 Tablespoons Instant coffee granules
- 1/2 cup Coffee liqueur
- 1/4 cup Crème de Cacao liqueur
- 3/4 cup Whipped cream
- 2 Tablespoons Semi-sweet chocolate, grated

Directions
a) In slow-cooker, combine hot water, coffee, and liqueurs.
b) Cover and heat on LOW 2-4 hours. Ladle into mugs or heat-proof glasses.
c) Top with whipped cream and grated chocolate.

85. Praline Coffee

Ingredients:
- 3 cups Hot brewed coffee
- 3/4 cups Half-and-half
- 3/4 cups Firmly packed Brown sugar
- 2 Tablespoons Butter or margarine
- 3/4 cup Praline liqueur
- Sweetened whipped cream

Directions

a) Cook first 4 Ingredients in a large saucepan over medium heat, stirring constantly, until Thoroughly heated, do not boil.

b) Stir in liqueur; serve with sweetened whipped cream.

86. Vodka Coffee

Ingredients:
- 2 cups Dark Brown Sugar-firmly packed
- 1 cup White Sugar
- 2 1/2 cups of Water
- 4 cups Pecan Pieces
- 4 Vanilla Beans split lengthwise
- 4 cups Vodka

Directions
a) Combine brown sugar, white sugar and water in saucepan over medium heat, until mixture starts to boil. Reduce heat and simmer 5 minutes.
b) Place vanilla beans and pecans into a large glass jar (as this makes 4 1/2 cups Pour hot mixture into jar and let cool. Add vodka
c) Cover tightly and store in a dark place. Turn jar over each day for the next 2 weeks to keep all ingredients combined. After 2 weeks, strain mixture, discarding solids.

87. Amaretto Cafe'

Ingredients:
- 1 1/2 cups Warm Water
- 1/3 cup Amaretto
- 1 Tablespoons Instant Coffee Crystals
- Whipped cream topping

Directions
a) Stir together water and instant coffee crystals in a microwavable dish.
b) Microwave uncovered, on 100% power for about 3 minutes or just till steaming hot.
c) Stir in the Amaretto. Serve in clear glass mugs. Top each mug of coffee mixture with some dessert topping.

88. Cafe Au Cin

Ingredients:
- 1 cup Cold Strong French roast coffee
- 2 Tablespoons Granulated sugar
- dash Cinnamon
- 2 oz. Tawny port
- 1/2 teaspoons Grated orange peel

Directions
a) Combine and mix in a blender at high speed.
b) Pour into chilled wine glasses.

89. Spiked Cappuccino

Ingredients:
- 1/2 cup Half-and-half
- 1/2 cup Freshly brewed espresso
- 2 Tablespoons Brandy
- 2 Tablespoons White rum
- 2 Tablespoons Dark crème de cacao
- Sugar

Directions
a) Whisk half-and-half in small saucepan over high heat until it becomes frothy, about 3 minutes.
b) Divide espresso coffee between 2 cups. Add half of the brandy and half of the crème de cacao to each cup.
c) Re-whisk half-and-half and pour into cups.
d) Sugar is optional

90. Gaelic Coffee

Ingredients:
- Black coffee; freshly made
- Scotch whiskey
- Raw brown sugar
- Real whipped cream; whipped until slightly thick

Directions
a) Pour the coffee into a warmed glass.
b) Add the whisky and brown sugar to taste. Stir well.
c) Pour some lightly whipped cream into the glass over the back of a teaspoon that is just above the top of the liquid in the cup.
d) It should float a bit.

91. Rye Whiskey Coffee

Ingredients:
- 1/4 cup Maple syrup; pure
- 1/2 cup Rye whiskey
- 3 cups Coffee; hot, black, double strength

Topping:
- 3/4 cup of Whipping cream
- 4 teaspoons Pure Maple syrup

Directions
a) Topping-Whip the 3/4 cup of whipped cream with the 4 teaspoons of Maple syrup until it forms a soft mound.
b) Divide maple syrup and whiskey among 4 pre-warmed heatproof glass mugs.
c) Pour in coffee to 1 inch from top.
d) Spoon topping over coffee.
e) Serve

92. Cherry Brandy Coffee

Ingredients:
- 1/2-ounce cherry brandy
- 5 ounces fresh black coffee
- 1 teaspoon sugar whipped cream
- Maraschino Cherry

Directions
a) Pour the coffee and Cherry brandy into a coffee cup, and add the sugar to sweeten.
b) Top with whipped cream and a maraschino cherry.

93. Danish Coffee

Ingredients:
- 8 c Hot coffee
- 1 c Dark rum
- 3/4 c Sugar
- 2 Cinnamon sticks
- 12 Cloves (whole)

Directions

a) In a very large heavy saucepan, combine all the Ingredients, cover and keep on low heat for about 2 hours.

b) Serve in coffee mugs.

94. Whiskey Shooter

Ingredients:
- 1/2 cups Skim milk
- 1/2 cups Plain low-fat yogurt
- 2 teaspoons Sugar
- 1 teaspoons Instant coffee powder
- 1 teaspoons Irish whiskey

Directions
a) Place all ingredients into a blender on low speed.
b) Blend until you can see that your Ingredients are incorporated into each other.
c) Use a tall shake glass for presentation.

95. Good Old Irish

Ingredients:
- 1.5 ounces Irish Cream Liqueur
- 1.5 ounces Irish Whiskey
- 1 cup hot brewed coffee
- 1 Tablespoons whipped cream
- 1 dash of nutmeg

Directions
a) In a coffee mug, combine Irish cream and The Irish Whiskey.
b) Fill mug with coffee. Top with a dollop of whipped cream.
c) Garnish with a sprinkle of Nutmeg.

96. Bushmills Irish Coffee

Ingredients:
- 1 1/2 ounces Bushmills Irish whiskey
- 1 teaspoons Brown sugar (optional)
- 1 dash Crème de menthe, green
- Extra Strong fresh coffee
- Whipped cream

Directions
a) Pour whiskey into Irish coffee cup and fill to 1/2 inch from top with coffee. Add sugar to taste and mix. Top with whipped cream and drizzle crème de menthe on top.
b) Dip rim of cup in sugar to coat edge.

97. Black Irish Coffee

Ingredients:
- 1 cups of strong Coffee
- 1 1/2 oz. Irish whisky
- 1 teaspoons Sugar
- 1 Tablespoons Whipped cream

Directions
a) Mix coffee, sugar, and whiskey in a large microwavable mug.
b) Microwave on high 1 to 2 minutes. Top with whipped cream
c) Careful when drinking, may need a moment to cool.

98. Creamy Irish Coffee

Ingredients:
- 1/3 cup Irish Cream Liqueur
- 1 1/2 cups Freshly Brewed Coffee
- 1/4 cup Heavy Cream, slightly sweetened and whipped

Directions
a) Divide the liqueur and coffee among 2 mugs.
b) Top with whipped cream.
c) Serve.

99. Old Fashioned Irish Coffee

Ingredients:
- 3/4 cup Warm Water
- 2 Tablespoons Irish Whiskey
- Dessert Topping
- 1 1/2 spoons Instant Coffee Crystals
- Brown Sugar to Taste

Directions
a) Combine water and instant coffee crystals. Microwave, uncovered, on
b) 100% power about 1 1/2 minutes or just till steaming hot. Stir in Irish whiskey and brown sugar.

100. Cream Liqueur Latte

Ingredients:
- 1-part Cream Liqueur
- 1½ parts Vodka

Directions
a) Shake with ice and strain into a Martini glass.
b) Enjoy

CONCLUSION

If you love coffee, then you'll love learning about the world of caffeinated drinks just waiting for you to try. Get global and get your caffeine fix with the collection of the most delicious recipes in this book. You'll find fun and unique ideas here for coffee-based beverages that you can enjoy at every meal. Whether you are looking for a new way to enjoy a morning cup or want to expand your knowledge of coffee customs, consider this your passport to caffeine heaven.